Wellington's Bone

The focus in this book is on past tense verbs.

Verbs ending with **-ed**

growled

wanted

picked

buried

decided

played

Verbs ending with **-ing**

going

bounding

guarding

Wellington had been given a
bone. He took it to his kennel.
He was not going to let
anybody touch his bone.

Kevin came bounding through
the farmyard gate. He ran up
to Wellington in the kennel.
Wellington growled at him.

Wellington wanted to be alone with his bone. He growled at Kevin as he picked up the bone and left his kennel.

He went into the garden. He sat down by a rose bush. He thought he would now enjoy his bone in peace.

Then he saw Jelly by the rose bush. He decided to bury his bone and have it later when everyone had gone away.

He dug a hole and he buried the bone. He put a stone on the soil to mark the spot. Then he sat down to guard it.

Kevin came into the garden. Wellington would not play. He growled at Kevin. Kevin went away to play with Jelly.

Wellington fell asleep guarding his bone. Meanwhile, Kevin and Jelly put some stones on the soil near Wellington.

Wellington woke up. He saw all the stones on the soil. Oh no! Where was his bone? He began to dig in the soil.

He could not find his bone. Kevin and Jelly had played a joke on him and now his bone was lost!

Words with digraphs used in this book

ay/ai:	away play played
a-e:	came gate later
ee/ea:	been asleep meanwhile peace
ie/i-e:	decided meanwhile
o-e:	hole rose bone alone stone woke joke
oo:	took
ou/ow:	bounding growled down now
er:	later
ar:	garden guard mark farmyard
aw:	saw
oi/oy:	enjoy soil
ear:	near